LOVE
WHERE THE
NIGHTS ARE
LONG CANADIAN LOVE POEMS

SELECTED BY IRVING LAYTON

DRAWINGS BY HAROLD TOWN

MCCLELLAND AND STEWART LIMITED

TORONTO/1962

0-7710-4851-3

DESIGNED BY FRANK NEWFELD

COVER PHOTOS: LAYTON/J. MAX
                      TOWN/P. POCOCK

PRINTED AND BOUND IN CANADA BY THE HUNTER ROSE COMPANY

CONTENTS

Love is surrender, concern, ecstasy. Bamboozled out of their wits and courage by the anti-life forces pressing against them, Canadians have forgotten this; but poets know that the great theme is love. Love's sweet torture transforms our grasping, unpleasant selves into tem= porary divinities and has us capering on the streets with the glory and arrogance of gods. It is the emotion that makes us endurable to one another; the flash so blinding that we cannot see wrinkles, grey hairs, skin pores, and all the other evidences of our pitiful mortality. It is the alchemist in our blood and gonads converting the shabby materials of our days and weeks into incandescent golden raptures, giving our cloddish lives lustre and grace. We are transformed, we walk taller; and our tears become triumphs, our cries of pain, hallelujahs, our mutterings of disappointment and failure, resounding choruses of praise. Love works on us the way great poetry does: it transports us out of our habitual selves and allows the angels to sweep new know= ledge into the vacated space. When we return we stand higher and better.

The death wish = bah! There is only the love wish, the desire in each of us for superabundant power and immortality. Analysts who preach fear and retreat to their victims, resignation and adjustment, can go to hell. So can Mrs Grundy and her numerous evil=smelling brood of censorious prigs, sniggering boobs, tight=lipped matrons, and frustrated nobodies found in all the cities, towns, and villages of this land. For these cannot endure the sight of people enjoying themselves, and impose their social unease and displeasure on the timorous in the hypocritical name of virtue, decency. Who has not seen their long, bony noses and glaring eyes ? Their prim, ascetic faces made pallid in the service of what they call righteous living? The really amazing thing is that they can still cow people into paying them respect, that so few have the courage to exclaim, "Let's cart them off to the booby=hatch!" Cart them away, I say, and all other botched individuals that with creed or convention would keep both young and old from the most human experience possible to them, the one that of all others makes them feel most intensely alive.

When Canadians are done with the excitements of professionalized sports and alcohol, a voice in their miserable, nightmarish souls tells them that contact, abandonment, passion, and the understanding heart are what matter most in our lives. Isolated from one another by the fears and repressions engendered in a materialistic society almost wholly given up to the worship of money and status; hoodwinked by egomaniacal poltroons among politicos and business executives; and robbed of their birthright of joy and intensity by any prude or long=faced puritan that can shake a finger at them, Canadians plead for compassion as no other people on earth. This is a cold country in more ways than one. The drag of middle=class mores is strongest here, for the mitigating forces of population, culture, heterogeneity are not sufficiently present to free the individual from the entangling coils of life=denying creeds and the inhibiting ideologies and customs of the dominant ethnic groups. He's caught early and stays trapped till the end of his days.

The Canadian is a born sucker for anything that will tie him up in knots. If a mediocrity is someone who unthinkingly lives by rules made for him by others, then this country can boldly lay claim to being a paradise for mediocrities. Here they will find no one great of heart or will to affront them = that's why it's a paradise! Can you imagine a Napoleon, or a Byron, or even a J. F. Kennedy living among us? We prefer the safe, the conventional, the unimaginative = the dull plodders whose fires were long ago quenched by hapless and thoroughly beaten schoolteachers and by repressed parents who think that sex is strictly for the birds. Yes, this is a cold country. Cold with the snow and frost that have entered into the bloodstream and packed ice around the heart; cold with fear, ignorance, repression, denial. Only alcohol con= sumed in great quantities can temporarily dissolve this hard pack of ice!

And yet Canadian poets have written some of the best love poetry in the world. When I wish to account for that fact, my reasoning goes some= thing like this: Canadians are a backward folk; they have not yet heard that love is dead. No runner from the big outside world has brought them the news from despairing Existentialist France or Marxist Russia whose leading poetic spokesman, Yevtushenko, has recently told us that Eros and economics should be made indistinguishably one = a lyric inserted in the laboured pages of *Das Kapital*. (I amuse myself by imagining the mockery of a Catullus or a Pushkin confronted by this robust pleb.) Our age, in the great centres of civilization, has bred narcissism, hysteria, anxiety, beatnikism; it has filled nostrils with the unmentionable odours of death, and increased the egocentricity of the individual whose first concern today is with himself and his own survival. Think of those sprawling megalopoli whose monstrous, un= stoppable advance converts fields and healthy forests into acres and acres of neurotics. Love cannot grow in this wreckage of human hopes, this junkyard; only psychoanalysis can, to explain why it doesn't. But Canada is not one of the great centres of civilization; we have no Negro problem to settle, no Algerian one; nor one of building up the perfect state by slaughtering fifteen million recalcitrant peasants; nor the problem of getting rid of colonies which we have ruled and exploited for centuries. In brief, we do not kill and mutilate and torture each other as is done in the more advanced countries of the world. The de= humanizing forces are not so irresistibly powerful here as they are, in the United States or Soviet Russia or Great Britain = not yet. They will, of course, mature and ripen in time and will be as devastating to Canadians as they have been to the denizens of New York, Moscow, and London. In the interval, however, our poets have been able to write of love as the grandest of human experiences and to turn to the everlasting poles of male and female for that intensification of life that alone can make the long, winter nights endurable.

And this is a country of vast, empty spaces. Desolation surrounds us, takes us in, fills our minds and hearts. We live with a white blankness nearly six months of each year. We can easily dissolve into it and dis= appear forever unless someone out of affection and concern holds us by the coattails and doesn't let go. In this vast, empty space, in this white blankness, love defines us, gives us a habitation and a name. More than others, our poets have known this to be true, and therefore their lyrics have a concreteness and particularity, an authenticity, unmatched by those of any other country.

> *There is a sorcerer in Lachine*
> *Who for a small fee will put a spell*
> *On my beloved*
>
> *Always I shall remember you, as my car moved*
> *Away from the station and left you alone by the gate*
> *Utterly and forever frozen in time and solitude*
> *Like a tree on the north shore of Lake Superior.*
>
> *At El Cortigo, with coffee*
> *tilting right and left*
>
> *Mrs McGonigle's boys enjoy the sun*
> *By gogglesful, and stare along the beach*

For the most part, love for these poets can never be the courtly play= thing it was for the Cavalier poets, an insincere frippery addressed to anonymous Cynthias and Lucastas. Were a Lovelace to appear among them he'd be laughed out of his affected simper quicker than one can say "gooseberries." Also not for them is the artificiality of the Italian and Spanish lyrists, or the witty highly wrought conceits of the English Metaphysicals. As for the French writers, they are much too rational and prosaic to believe in love = except as a disease of the mind which ought to be analysed minutely and compassionately. Their best poets when they write about love may convince themselves; they somehow never convince me. At most they strike me as wanting very hard to believe in the glories they claim to have felt and seen. But after all, what can grocers selling herrings and pepper know about the exalta= tions of love ? Or the avaricious peasants of Burgundy ? Or the dreary Existentialists of Paris ? The French are a cold, egocentric, logical people: long ago love was murdered there. It is its ghost, romance, in all its poor glitter that haunts those purlieus; and sensuality, which the vanity of the Frenchman wishes to fob off on the world as the highest reach of human wisdom.

In the writings of the older Canadian poets and of my contemporaries I have sought mainly for those extreme statements of surrender = for that, after all, is what love is all about: when the ego forgets its strategies of protection or retreat and men and women stand naked, revealed in all their clotheless glory. These are the poems that can make us forget the absurd homunculi among us: the censors, the shuffling politicians, the prudes and puritans, the hyperborean life=deniers and nay=sayers. In them Mrs Grundy and her brood get drowned and stay that way. These poems also enable us to forget the mechanical routines of a nine=to=five existence endured by the majority of diminished Canadians. Only the poet can seize that moment, most joyful and significant in the lives of each, to confer on it the dignity of the eternal. Henceforth every bank clerk, salesgirl, typist, gatekeeper, prostitute, firechief, business tycoon, rabbi, school principal, and nurse walks under the white, stainless radiance which these poems shed over them. For out of the darkness and snow and mist and rain, out of the cold, climatic and human, out of the comfortless alienation, have come these astonishing words of surrender and ecstasy.

Beyond illusion, cynicism, mawkishness, despair, even divinity itself, I have looked for poems that gave me the bare bone and marrow of the

individual. I wanted to hear the unmistakable cry of rapture and suffer=
ing; I wanted to hear it clear and unmuffled. Love: adolescent or adult=
erous; tender or brutal; obscene, lustful, visionary, animal. Love:
anarchic or responsible, sacramental or earthy; destroyer and preserver
of conventions, rigidities, artifacts; paradox and riddle. Love, that
cohabiting with death, brings forth art. And the cry at that moment
when love turns into contempt and hate, when going sour in the
mouth it turns into discord, the desire to hurt and humiliate. I wanted
to hear the love cry of men and women exposed and defenceless, all
coverings tossed aside with disdain or dignity as ridiculous encum=
brances. For the love cry is the most perplexing of all since it is the
most truly human = bawdy, wanton, sacrificial, selfish, humbling, ex=
alting, coarse, angelic = for it is the one cry that by its variety and
meaningfulness abashes the gods themselves in their bland heavens
and makes them envious of the turbulent sons and daughters of men.

As the Mist Leaves No Scar

As the mist leaves no scar
On the dark green hill,
So my body leaves no scar
On you, nor ever will.

When wind and hawk encounter,
What remains to keep ?
So you and I encounter,
Then turn, then fall to sleep.

As many nights endure
Without a moon or star,
So will we endure
When one is gone and far.

Sacrament by the Water

How shall I sing the accomplished waters
Whose teeming cells make green my hopes
How shall the Sun at daybreak marry us
Twirling these waters like a hoop.

Gift of the waters that sing
Their eternal passion for the sky,
Your exact beauty in a wave of tumult
Drops an Eden about your thighs.

Green is the singing singing water
And green is every joyous leaf
White myrtle's in your hand and in the other
The hairy apple bringing life.

Canadian Love Song

Your body's a small word with many meanings.
Love. If. Yes. But. Death.
Surely I will love you a little while,
perhaps as long as I have breath.

December is thirteen months long.
July's one afternoon; therefore
lovers must outwit wool,
learn how to puncture fur.

To my love's bed, to keep her warm,
I'll carry wrapped and heated stones.
That which is comfort to the flesh
is sometimes torture to the bones.

I Loved Thee, Atthis

I loved thee, Atthis, in the long ago,
When the great oleanders were in flower
In the broad herded meadows full of sun.
And we would often at the fall of dusk
Wander together by the silver stream,
When the soft grass=heads were all wet with dew
And purple=misted in the fading light.
And joy I knew and sorrow at thy voice,
And the superb magnificence of love =
The loneliness that saddens solitude,
And the sweet speech that makes it durable =
The bitter longing and the keen desire,
The sweet companionship through quiet days
In the slow ample beauty of the world,
And the unutterable glad release
Within the temple of the holy night.
O Atthis, how I loved thee long ago
In that fair perished summer by the sea!

Celebration

When you kneel below me
and in both your hands
hold my manhood like a sceptre,

When you wrap your tongue
about the amber jewel
and urge my blessing,

I understand those Roman girls
who danced around a shaft of stone
and kissed it till the stone was warm.

Kneel, love, a thousand feet below me,
so far I can barely see your mouth and hands
perform the ceremony,

Kneel till I topple to your back
with a groan, like those gods on the roof
that Samson pulled down.

Interval

Searching for the point where rivers meet
Or the door that leads into a lighted room,
He thought he found in woman a divining rod
That knows where all the treasure's hidden.
He thought her flesh was touched with lightning
Or magic impulses that guess how rivers meet.
In her hands he saw the golden key
To vistas of unending green, blinding
The enemies of his unity.

He learned otherwise under a summer sky,
Embracing her one day when change of trains
Left them an hour or two to kill, they fled the town
Came to a field = after the rain it was =
The ground fresh and black, the last cherries
Withering on bushes, and dried raspberries
Clinging to fences, a sleepy cow in pasture
The distant rumble of freight cars
Heading for city.

They lay down together and they kissed
And in that kiss he felt his past defeats
Narrow and bind him and his dream grown large
Filled the light sky to its cloudiest limits,
Stretched like a bubble and as quickly broke.
The dream fell and gave him back
Himself in a thousand pieces
All separate and disjointed.
Then he knew there is no golden key,
No one has hidden it, there is no joyous room
Where man completes his marriage in a moment,
There are no easy signposts, only a lonely road
That each one travels with his suffering.

After Dark

Perhaps because I've had so much of my love
in the shadow of parks, on cold=lipped sands of beaches,
anywhere two bodies could lie, be close together, where hands
      could reach out
to feel the fond, desired flesh, anywhere under sweep of trees,
      smell of grass, that they could know
earth's nearness, mute sympathy, wind=whispered blessing,
and be not afraid
of the peeping=tom public eye, all the polared thoughts of its
      steadily shrivelling
inch of mind, never easily measured =

maybe because of this
I feel kinship, like brother or sister,
for these young bodies sprawled tonight in the lie of their loving,
legs curled, soft roundness of them, sweet torture that transforms
      them, that pushes them above
work at the office, banal situations, long empty hours of their
      lives:

and walk past them quietly, a little wistfully, looking straight
      ahead,
my footsteps seeming somehow to sound *alone* . . .

Shore Leave

Look = my love, you've lit up the country.
What will you do with so many stars ?
How would you have me
Shy as a maiden,
Or slut from a brothel
Paid for the night ?

You're fresh as sea spray, handsome sailor;
Muscles hard with ship=deck chores.
Yet how gently you dress me
With tender caresses,
Till I'd have you touch me
Gently no more.

Should I feel shame in the heat of your loving ?
Turn on the lights = see, my eyes are clear.
What other purpose have I a body
Than to share
In your pleasures,
Add spice to the game ?

I'd pay a penance if I kept silent,
Pursed my mouth in a tight cruel smile.
Should I offer you quotas in frozen ice ?
Tonight I'm your plaything =
A slave girl you purchased.
Tomorrow I'll be your wife.

At El Cortijo

At El Cortijo, with coffee
tilting right and left
in talk weird as alcohol,
a little dark one backed
into my knee, didn't
look round . . . just sat on it.

No introduction! She took
my femur for a public perch,
and in that exhilarant
fluctuation of conversation
quivered
like a kitten ready to bounce.

I wrung myself with love
for the finely wound nerve of her,
balanced there,
and the way loose hairs
half=twisted
at her palpitating nape.

Disturbed by my rude eye
she twitched round to glare
my grin into a grimace,
then looked back
but didn't budge
her delicate handful of bum.

Eurynome

Come all old maids that are squeamish
And afraid to make mistakes,
Don't clutter your lives up with boyfriends:
The nicest girls marry snakes.

If you don't mind slime on your pillow
And caresses as gliding as ice
= Cold skin, warm heart, remember,
And besides, they keep down the mice =

If you're really serious= minded,
It's the best advice you can take:
No rumpling, no sweating, no nonsense,
Oh who would not sleep with a snake ?

Rapture

Sweet lovers lie around the bay
Lapped in each other's arms;
Mrs Beleek with Dr Gay,
Joad with Miss Decharmes,
Snug in their cabins tucked away
Sleeping the early hours of day.

Fishes within the burnished bay
Dimple the face thereof
Leaping to enter, as they may,
The mirror world above.
Delicate fishes, how they play!
Rapture is in the air today.

Old Song

Since nothing so much is
as the present kiss
don't let an old kiss
so disconcert you,
but know it is no crime
to give a new kiss time
and reason to convert you.

The first you ever had
was an eternal lad
whose smile was very May
no other mouth replaces,
but this today
has an October way
to harvest his embraces.

Loves are the fruits of time
different and the same
the perfect and imperfect,
and in the body's branches
where old kisses hang
and sweet birds sang
the wind fills his paunches.

And any kiss at all
is present after all
for now is all we have
now when we want them,
so grant your kisses leave
to give and to receive
nor waste your lips to count them.

Song

I almost went to bed
without remembering
the four white violets
I put in the buttonhole
of your green sweater

and how I kissed you then
and you kissed me
shy as though I'd
never been your lover

Villanelle

My love and yours must be enjoyed alone:
My sleeping sister and infernal twin,
I know your body better than my own.

Only the natural conscience of the bone
Protests the sadness of the dream wherein
My love and yours must be enjoyed alone;

But the body has reasons to the soul unknown:
The soul of another is dark, said Augustine;
I know your body better than my own.

You that know everything that can be known,
Tell me through what punishment of what sin
My love and yours must be enjoyed alone?

Why has the darkness and the distance grown,
Why do we fear to let the stranger in?
= I know your body better than my own,

I know the lamp is out, the bird has flown . . .
To find that end where other loves begin
My love and yours must be enjoyed alone:
I know your body better than my own.

The Widower

Not lonely now in bed the widower lies
Who late at night has felt the smooth=skinned swell
Of rounded sheets arouse his skin to flame
Or in his dreams, like Ixion in hell,
Has clasped a curve of softness that became
A cloudy pillow to his morning eyes.
Such nightmare waking not tonight applies;
It is warm flesh that meets his warmer thighs.

Warm flesh and tendered in such tender wise
He feels his love return and all the black
Life=loneliness lie conquered on its back
There in the dark one passion=breathing space
Before his mind recalls the raddled face
Of his love=machine and her hard, glazed eyes.

Will to Win

Your tall French legs, my V for victory,
My sign and symphony, Eroica,
Uphold me in these days of my occupation
And stir my underground resistance.

Crushed by the insidious infiltration of routine
I was wholly overrun and quite cut off.
The secret agents of my daily detail
Had my capital city under their rule and thumb.

Only a handful of me escaped to the hillside,
Your side, my sweet and holy inside,
And cowering there for a moment I drew breath,
Grew solid as trees, took root in a fertile soil.

Here by my hidden fires, drop your supplies =
Love, insight, sensibility, and myth =
Thousands of fragments rally to my cause,
I ride like Joan to conquer my whole man.

The Day Aviva Came to Paris

The day you came naked to Paris
The tourists returned home without their guide books,
The hunger in their cameras finally appeased.

Alone once more with their gargoyles, the Frenchmen
Marvelled at the imagination that had produced them
And once again invited terror into their apéritifs.
Death was no longer exiled to the cemeteries.

In their royal gardens where the fish die of old age,
They perused something else besides newspapers
= A volume perhaps by one of their famous writers.
They opened their hearts to let your tender smile defrost them;
Their livers filled with an unassuageable love of justice.
They became the atmosphere around them.

They learned to take money from the Americans
Without a feeling of revulsion towards them;
And to think of themselves
As not excessively subtle or witty.
"Au diable with Voltaire," they muttered,
"Who was a national calamity."
Au diable with la République.
(A race of incurable petits bourgeois, the French
Are happiest under a horse under a man)
Au diable with la Monarchie!
We saw no goddesses during either folly;
Our bald=headed savants never had told us
Such a blaze of pubic hair anywhere existed."

And they ordered the grandson of Grandma Moses
To paint it large on the dome of le Sacré=Coeur.

My little one, as if under those painted skies
It was again 1848,
They leaped as one mad colossal Frenchman from their café Pernods
Shouting, "Vive L'Australienne!
Vive Layton who brought her among us!
Let us erect monuments of black porphyry to them!
Let us bury them in the Panthéon!"

(Pas si vite, messieurs; we are still alive)

And when, an undraped Jewish Venus,
You pointed to a child, a whole slum starving in her eyes,
Within earshot of the Tuileries,
The French who are crazy or catholic enough
To place, facing each other, two tableaux
= One for the Men of the Convention, and one puffing the
                              Orators of the Restoration =
At once made a circle wide as the sky around you
While the Mayor of the 5th Arondissement
Addressed the milling millions of Frenchmen:

"See how shapely small her adorable ass is;
Of what an incredible pink rotundity each cheek.
A bas Merovingian and Valois!
A bas Charlemagne and Henri Quatre!
For all the adulations we have paid them
In our fabulous histoires
They cannot raise an erection between them. Ah,
For too long has the madness of love
Been explained to us by sensualists and curés.
A bas Stendhal! A bas Bossuet!

"Forever and forever, from this blazing hour
All Paris radiates from Aviva's nest of hair
= Delicate hatchery of profound delights =
From her ever=to=be adored Arche de Triomphe!
All the languors of history
Take on meaning clear as a wineglass or the belch of an angel
Only if thought of as rushing
On the wings of a rhinoceros towards this absorbing event.
Voyeurs, voyez! The moisture of her instep
Is a pool of love
Into which sheathed in candy=paper
Anaesthetized politicians drop from the skies!"
(Word jugglery of course, my Sweet; but the French love it
= Mistake it in fact for poetry)

And the applaudissements and bravos
Bombinating along the Boulevard Saint=Germain
Make the poor docile Seine
Think our great Atlantic was upon it.
It overflowed with fright into the bookstalls
And sidewalk cafés.
Fifteen remaining Allemands with their cameras
Were flushed down the Rue Pigalle.

And when you were raised up
Into my hairy arms by the raving emotional crowds
Waving frenzied bottles of Beaujolais
And throwing the corks away ecstatically
(Not saving them!)
It was my Love, my Darling,
As if someone had again ordered an advance
Upon the Bastille
Which we recalled joyously, face to face at last,
Had yielded after only a small token resistance.

Looking for Nancy

Looking for Nancy
        everywhere, I've stopped
girls in trenchcoats
and blue dresses,
        said
Nancy I've looked
        all over
        hell for you,
Nancy I've been afraid
that I'd die
before I found you.

        But there's always
        been some mistake:

a broken streetlight,
too much rum or merely
my wanting too much
for it to be her.

Philander's Song

I sat and read Anacreon.
  Moved by the gay, delicious measure
I mused that lips were made for love,
  And love to charm a poet's leisure.

And as I mused a maid came by
  With something in her look that caught me.
Forgotten was Anacreon's line,
  But not the lesson he had taught me.

Steps of Love

Coming out of your clothes you were
girl in the night
                    naked in a strange house
                    receptive to a question
                    of what I would do

you were for the first time
uncovered to me
your two white shoulders thin in the air
hunched & shining there

& breast turning to me
cool skin of unimagined girl suspended in shadow
& hands now bashful
searching for a place to rest behind you

                    You listened to my silence

                    you gathered something in your mind

                    and you danced on your bare feet

                    with your long arms to meet me

My Lady Can Sleep

My lady can sleep
Upon a handkerchief
Or if it be Fall
Upon a fallen leaf.

I have seen the hunters
Kneel before her hem =
Even in her sleep
She turns away from them.

The only gift they offer
Is their abiding grief =
I pull out my pockets
For a handkerchief or leaf.

The Sailor's Sweetheart

O if love were had for asking,
In the markets of the town,
Hardly a lass would think to wear
A fine silken gown:
But love is had by grieving
By choosing and by leaving,
And there's no one to ask me
If heavy lies my heart.

O if love were had for a deep wish
In the darkness of the night,
There'd be a truce to longing
Between the dusk and the light:
But love is had for sighing,
For living and for dying,
And there's no one to ask me
If heavy lies my heart.

O if love were had for taking
Like honey from the hive,
The bees that made the tender stuff
Could hardly keep alive:
But love it is a wounded thing,
A tremor and a smart,
And there's no one left to kiss me now
Over my heavy heart.

The Cuckold's Song

If this looks like a poem
I might as well warn you at the beginning
that it's not meant to be one.
I don't want to turn anything into poetry.
I know all about her part in it
but I'm not concerned with that right now.
That is between you and me.
Personally I don't give a damn who led who on:
in fact I wonder if I give a damn at all.
But a man's got to say something.
Anyhow you fed her 5 MacKewan Ales,
took her to your room, put the right records on,
and in an hour or two it was done.
I know all about passion and honour
but unfortunately this had really nothing to do with either:
oh there was passion I'm only too sure
and even a little honour
but the important thing was to cuckold Leonard Cohen.
Hell, I might just as well address this to both of you:
I haven't time to write anything else.
I've got to say my prayers.
I've got to wait by the window.
I repeat: the important thing was to cuckold Leonard Cohen.
I like that line because it's got my name in it.
What really makes me sick
is that everything goes on as it went before:
I'm still a sort of friend,
I'm still a sort of lover.

But not for long:
that's why I'm telling this to the two of you.
The fact is I'm turning to gold, turning to gold.
It's a long process, they say,
it happens in stages.
This is to inform you that I've already turned to clay.

City Song

Come, let us take the air
And stop the bus and pay the fare,

Drink sweetly of city streets
And dream of love on upper seats.

Summer has broken on this town
Has blossomed gold on concrete lawn

Broken gold in lovers' veins,
Smashed the million windowpanes.

And when the summer sun is set,
On the sidewalk we shall sit

In kitchen chairs and listen to
The radio that sings for you

And you, my love, shall watch with me
The uptown strip of galaxy

Neon semaphore the dawn
Above the roof when stars are done

O live with me and you shall have
The sun to sack, stars to thieve

For to my heart is come
Summer's epithalamium.

The Garden of the Sexes

I have a garden closed away
And shadowed from the light of day
Where Love hangs bound on every tree
And I alone go free.

His sighs, that turn the weathers round,
His tears, that water all the ground,
His blood, that reddens in the vine,
These all are mine.

At night the golden apple=tree
Is my fixed station, whence I see
Terrible, sublime and free,
My loves go wheeling over me.

Dark Around Light

How to wipe the night away
to wish the sunrise in
that is in you
                This beleaguers me
lying here alone
the phone
            under my hand
a whole city of night
        between us

My desklamp is on the table beside me
its light is turned back
                        by the window
I've promised not to call you =
I cannot write =
All the couriers die in their tracks =
The night is not out there =
        is it

Is it
darkness out there ?
Is there nothing but darkness
      between us

Then I can run through the streets
poking flashlight light
into the road before me
waving the torch around
wiping away the night

Or I can pick up the telephone
and whisper into your ear
call you and promise no more
call to you
      and wipe the night away

Song of the Impermanent Husband

Oh I would
          I would in a minute
if the cusswords and bitter anger couldn't =
if the either/or quarrel didn't =
and the fat around my middle wasn't =
if I was young if
               I wasn't so damn sure
I couldn't find another maddening bitch
like you holding on for dear life to
all the different parts of me for
twenty or twenty
             thousand years
I'd leave in the night like
a disgraced caviar salesman
                 descend the moonlight
stairs to Halifax
  (uh = no = not Halifax
well then Toronto
             uh
I guess not Toronto either/or
nouveau riche Vancouver down
             down
                down

the dark stairs to
the South Seas' sunlit milky reefs and
        the jungle's green
                unending bank account with
all the brown girls being brown
                as they can be and all
the one piece behinds stretched tight tonight
in small sarongs not to be touched though Oh
beautiful as an angel's ass without the genitals
and me
        in Paris like a smudged Canadian postcard and
(dear me)
        all the importuning white=and=lily girls
of Rue Pigalle
                stroll
the sodden London streets and
                find a sullen foggy woman who
enjoyed my odd colonial ways and send
a postcard back to you about my faithfulness and
talk about the lovely lovely English weather
I'd be the slimiest most uxorious wife deserter
                my shrunk amoeba self absurd inside
a saffron girl's geography and

hating me between magnetic nipples
but
     fooling no one in all the sad
     and much emancipated world
Why then I'll stay at least for tea for
all the brownness is too brown and
all the whiteness too damned white
and I'm afraid
              afraid of being
any other woman's man who
might be me
        afraid the
unctuous and uneasy self I glimpse
sometimes might lose my faint and yapping cry for
being anything was never quite what I intended
And you you
        bitch no irritating
questions re love and permanence only
        an unrolling lifetime here
between your rocking thighs and
        the semblance of motion

Field of Long Grass

When she walks in the field of long grass
The delicate little hands of the grass
Lean forward a little to touch her.

Light is like the waving of the long grass.
Light is the faint to and fro of her dress.
Light rests for a while in her bosom.

When it is all gone from her bosom's hollow
And out of the field of long grass,
She walks in the dark by the edge of the fallow land.

Then she begins to walk in my heart.
Then she walks in me, swaying in my veins.

My wrists are a field of long grass
A little wind is kissing.

For the Bridegroom Coming Out of His Chamber

The young men with the sparse beards laud the bride;
"She puts no rouges to her lips; no small
Black beauty spots upon her cheeks; no pall
Of perfumed dust upon her neck; no dyed
Resplendence on her lovely head; no pride
Of henna on her fingernails at all;
Yet is she very beautiful withal,
Most beautiful yet not beautified."
The long=haired virgins musically doff
Their silence, and around the bridegroom wheel,
Singing his bride and all the seven days' love
That will be hers anon, the nuptial weal
That he will serve; in evidence thereof
He breaks the wineglass underneath his heel.

Letter in Late September

Mornings
the postman's footfall
and crackling leaves
wake me.

I water empty flowerpots
bandage rosebush stumps
and sever rotting limbs
from the elm
sighing over my skylight.

Nights
my body longs
for your return
and my dreams ridicule me.

Even my poems
are fruitless
and wither
with cumulus regrets.

The New Mattress

Where once the long valley was
that I rolled down
to the twin towns of your breasts,
to the unpredictable
suburbs of your thighs,

is now a plain,
flat and monotonous,
and I don't much like travelling
such usual countryside.

The Bishopric

Yes, and finding my small friar
sullen, cowled and scowling
in his beggar's posture:

Ha, my voice went sour
for the college girl squirming
under my length of form.
"I must reread my own poems,"
I said bitterly. "Or so it seems."

"Luckily for you," she breathed,
"no one will ever believe this
= not even your worst biographer."

I roared and that did it.
There was an instant election
as she brought her youthful face,
laughing,
into the sweet diocese of my body.

Elaine in a Bikini

Mrs McGonigle's boys enjoy the sun
By gogglesful, and stare along the beach
Whose innocence is almost all Elaine,
   Almost, but not quite, all.

Felicitously she comes in every eye
Bending her knees and tender finger nails
While the incalculable strings gather in
   What's hers to gather in.

Her feet entice themselves across the sands
Down to the water's edge, and the old sea
Fumbles about the naked afternoon
   As though in paradise.

I am felicitous too on the bright shore
Waiting for darkness with the roving boys
And all but gathered in myself with strings,
   What's mine to gather in.

Winter Love

Before we go
    Roll with me once more
Across the snow
    For we are dressed and hot.

Put your parka arms
    Around my neck at once,
Your legs between mine
    And twisted in tightly.

I move fingers into
    Your steaming soft body
Beneath a coat of wool
    Then we sigh together.

As we turn over
    Glimpse if you can
The sugared pines
    Coming to a prong.

They are lovely
    And I see them
Through your silver breath
    By love=shot eyes.

Roll with me again
    For I love your weight
Pressing on mine
    Over and over again.

Cape Breton Summer Evening

The band isn't worth a damn
and the sweat is working through her powder
through the starch of his carefully ironed shirt.

Outside the moon
sends old ghosts to walk a thoroughfare of gold
across the water=white beach to driftwood shore. A breeze runs
smelling deep lake and pine branch.

Thank God for intermissions!

Our limbs ache with desire, heat's in our blood,
as we climb the wood road till the forest takes us,
leaving the loud lights, the chattering,
and our friends of the dance floor guzzling pop and piercing
the sad skins of hotdogs.

Duet

Let me dance for you my hallowed gentlemen.
These are not tits, they are breasts.
A dual personality.
With these your mother satisfied your infant hunger,
My confirmation of your aesthetic pleasure.
Hips are part of my anatomy.
The pelvis that originally supported you
Still contains the fever of life.
Rhythm = the pulse of your proven manhood.
I will not abuse your imagination.
I ask you not to abuse mine.
The derision of your unsuccessful attainments
Is not contained in my woman,
Prescribed by your sex.
Our project is not only love.
Your whistles paint the make=up on our faces,
Silly fillies = we are taught it is a man's world,
And lift our skirts another inch.
I will dance for you my hallowed gentlemen,
When one of you can dance as well for me.

The Sorcerer

There is a sorcerer in Lachine
Who for a small fee will put a spell
On my beloved, who has sea=green
Eyes, and on my doting self as well.

He will transform us, if we like, to goldfish:
We shall swim in a crystal bowl,
And the bright water will go swish
Over our naked bodies; we shall have no soul.

In the morning the syrupy sunshine
Will dance on our tails and fins.
I shall have her then all for mine,
And Father Lebeau will hear no more of her sins.

Come along, good sir, change us into goldfish.
I would put away intellect and lust,
Be but a red gleam in a crystal dish,
But kin of the trembling ocean, not of the dust.

Divinity

Were I a clumsy poet
I'd compare you to Helen;
Ransack the mythologies
Greek, Chinese, and Persian

For a goddess vehement
And slim; one with form as fair.
Yet find none. O, Love, you are
Lithe as a Jew peddler

And full of grace. Such lightness
Is in your step, instruments
I keep for the beholder
To prove you walk, not dance.

Merely to touch you is fire
In my head; my hair becomes
A burning bush. When you speak,
Like Moses I am dumb

With marvelling, or like him
I stutter with pride and fear:
I hold, Love, divinity
In my changed face and hair.

"*I Will Arise and Go Now*"

Let's borrow a tent and live on The North Shore
Where the wind beats bluff from Labrador
And summer flutters by at half mast,
Cut the umbilical cord of the past
While our out=of=work benefits last.

The hungry ? Let's not appease them.
If they had the power
They'd only make you paint to please them
And me punctuate my poetry.
Let's not mean, but be.

Let's sign a ban=the=bomb petition
To show we're intelligent
Then let politics go to perdition,
While you tell me and I'll tell you·
How sweet we are.

I will read you Henry Miller
And you'll wear your diaphragm.
Selling out the future
And owning no geiger counter,
Let's take it on the lam.

The Desiring Heart

Well I found you in the twilit garden,
Laid a lover's hand upon your shoulder,
And we both were made aware of loving
Past the reach of reason to unravel,
Or the much desiring heart to follow.

There we heard the breath among the grasses
And the gurgle of soft=running water,
Well contented with the spacious starlight,
The cool wind's touch and the deep blue distance,
Till the dawn came in with golden sandals.

Eros and Psyche

How love was fought out
and the things we did:
      your slight thighs pressed
in that struggle, fought to be self=contained, man=proof,
then clenched, unclenched, were given
      all raddled with desire.

Or other times, together
    wanting in the cold bed what only each could give,
your thighs learned to move
willingly always when the time came. Now

we enter that play like two athletes
your legs locked about my impalpable knees
      and cannot hold that tryst
tight or long enough to prove
how at one your and my ghost are in this.

Executions

the beauty of women clatters upon me
their slanted ankles at street corners
stampede me to bits as they laugh
through their ingenious hair the wind
blows my heart into a buzz saw
rampant amid my flesh and bone

one half= smile or one casually aimed eye
boom I am run down by heavy traffic
the beauty of women flickered through bus windows
hands in black gloves and pensive mouths
grinds me like a coffee bean

I would offer my life to unreal gods
to speculations in serene bibliotecs
but the librarian has tropical breasts
and I crash from them as from a cliff

the beauty of women applying lipstick
drowns me in blood
their compacts click shut and whish
my head drops into the basket

Song for a Late Hour

No one told me
to beware your bracelets,
the winds I could expect
from your small breasts.
No one told me
the tumult of your hair.
When a lock touched me
I knew the sensations
of shattering glass.

Your kissings put
blue waters around me.
I would look at you
with bold Cretan mirth:
I would forget
I am a cringing Semite,
a spaniel suffering
about your tight skirts.

I slabber for your rippling
hips, your white shoulders.
I am sick
with love of you. Girl, o girl,
let our washed limbs make
a perverse Star of David
and cones of flesh,
Cythera all night
at my silvered back.

From the Hazel Bough

He met a lady
on a lazy street
hazel eyes
and little plush feet

her legs swam by
like lovely trout
eyes were trees
where boys leant out

hands in the dark and
a river side
round breasts rising
with the finger's tide

she was plump as a finch
and live as a salmon
gay as silk and
proud as a brahmin

they winked when they met
and laughed when they parted
never took time
to be brokenhearted

but no man sees
where the trout lie now
or what leans out
from the hazel bough

Ferris Wheel

Clothespinned to your halo
hang the smutty socks
of my love.

When you turn
your head, dear,
you make an amazing
ferris wheel.

Adolescence

In love they wore themselves in a green embrace.
A silken rain fell through the spring upon them.
In the park she fed the swans and he
whittled nervously with his strange hands.
And white was mixed with all their colours
as if they drew it from flowering trees.

At night his two=finger whistle brought her down
the waterfall stairs to his shy smile
which, like an eddy, turned her round and round
lazily and slowly so her will
was nowhere = as in dreams things are and aren't.

Walking along the avenues in the dark
street lamps sang like sopranos in their heads
with a violence they never understood
and all their movements when they were together
had no conclusion.

Only leaning into the question had they motion:
after they parted were savage and swift as gulls.
Asking and asking the hostile emptiness
they were as sharp as partly sculptured stone
and all who watched, forgetting, were amazed
to see them form and fade before their eyes.

Ersatz

Kiss her, kiss her, kiss her a thousand times,
over and over rub your cheek to her cheek, feel
    it burn you, hot as the lips of flame,
finger her breasts almost savagely, till they seem
    to grow in your hands.

Then for a moment body to body still,
eyes in the dark watching the snow's gleam
under the streetlight there beyond the window,

wonder why it's not the same, why it's no good, no
    good at all,
and how long, you, can you go on fooling yourself
    about the others,
how long before the emptiness will go, or will it always
keep on killing and aching and crying here in the
    darkness.

To Anthea

When I no more shall feel the sun,
    Nor taste the salt brine on my lips;
    When one to me are stinging whips
And rose leaves falling one by one;

I shall forget your little ears
    And your crisp hair and violet eyes;
    And all your kisses and your lies
Will be as futile as your tears.

R. I. P.

How do you think we'll rest
With tombstones on our chest?
I had rather recline
With your breast on mine,
    Love, on violets.

Or how shall we know peace
Broken piece by piece
In decay? I'd rather fret
Now for what I get
    From lips like these,

And leave nothing to wish
When we've become a dish
For the worms, my friend.
Leave them, hot heart, at end
    Cold cuts to finish.

Departure

Always I shall remember you, as my car moved
Away from the station and left you alone by the gate
Utterly and forever frozen in time and solitude
Like a tree on the north shore of Lake Superior.
It was a moment only, and you were gone,
And I was gone, and we and it were gone,
And the two parts of the enormous whole we had known
Melted and swirled away in their separate streams
Down the smooth, granite slope of our watershed.

We shall find, each, the deep sea in the end,
A stillness, and a movement only of tides
That wash a world, whole continents between,
Flooding the estuaries of alien lands.
And we shall know, after the flow and ebb,
Things central, absolute and whole.
Brought clear of silt, into the open roads,
Events shall pass like waves, and we shall stay.

Acknowledgements

We wish to thank the following authors, publishers, and copyright holders for their kind permission to reproduce the poems in this book.

Earle Birney, for "From the Hazel Bough."

George Bowering, for "Dark Around Light" and "Steps of Love."

Avi Boxer, for "Ferris Wheel," originally published in *Artisan*, and "Letter in Late September," originally published in *Delta*.

Louis Dudek, for "Eros and Psyche," "Old Song," and "R.I.P."

Ralph Gustafson, for "City Song," from *Flight into Darkness*, Pantheon Books, New York.

The Hawkshead Press and Milton Acorn, for "I Will Arise and Go Now," from *Against a League of Liars*.

Jewish Publication Society of America and A. M. Klein, for "For the Bridegroom Coming Out of His Chamber," from *Poems*.

George Johnston, for "Rapture," originally published in *The New Yorker*.

Gertrude Katz, for "Duet," originally published in *The Fiddlehead*, and "Shore Leave," originally published in *Poems for 27 cents*.

Malcolm Miller, for "Executions."

McClelland and Stewart Limited, for "The Desiring Heart" and "I Loved Thee, Atthis" from *Sappho* by Bliss Carman.

McClelland and Stewart Limited and Leonard Cohen, for "As the Mist Leaves No Scar," "Celebration," "The Cuckold's Song," "My Lady Can Sleep," and "Song" from *The Spice-Box of Earth*.

McClelland and Stewart Limited and John Glassco, for "Villanelle," from *The Deficit Made Flesh*.

McClelland and Stewart Limited and Irving Layton, for "Divinity," "Sacrament by the Water," and "Song for a Late Hour," from *A Red Carpet for the Sun*"; "The Day Aviva Came to Paris," from *The Swinging Flesh;* "The Bishopric," from *Balls for a One-Armed Juggler*.

Henry Moscovitch, for "Winter Love."

Alden Nowlan and *The Fiddlehead*, for "Canadian Love Song" and "Looking for Nancy."

Oxford University Press and George Johnston, for "Elaine in a Bikini," from *The Cruising Auk*.

Oxford University Press and Jay Macpherson, for "Eurynome " and "The Garden of the Sexes," from *The Boatman*.

Oxford University Press and A. J. M. Smith, for "Field of Long Grass,"
"The Sorcerer," and "To Anthea," from *Collected Poems*.

P. K. Page, for "Adolescence."

A. W. Purdy, for "Song of the Impermanent Husband."

The Ryerson Press and Milton Acorn, for "At El Cortijo," from *The Brain's
the Target*.

The Ryerson Press and Fred Cogswell, for "The Widower," from *Descent
from Eden*.

The Ryerson Press, for "Philander's Song" by Sir Charles G. D. Roberts,
from *The Selected Poems of Sir Charles G. D. Roberts;* and for "The
Sailor's Sweetheart" by Duncan Campbell Scott, from *The Selected Poems
of Duncan Campbell Scott*.

The Ryerson Press and F. R. Scott, for "Departure" and "Will to Win,"
from *Events and Signals*.

The Ryerson Press and Miriam Waddington, for "Interval," from *The Second
Silence*.

Raymond Souster, for "After Dark," "Cape Breton Summer Evening,"
"Ersatz," and "The New Mattress."